To
The Lattimore girls

From
Judy Cradoak

2022

INTRODUCTION

Gizmo was a kitty that belonged to my late son, Timothy who lived next door to me. After my son unexpectedly passed away Christy, his daughter, took Gizmo away to a different city to live with her mom and a house full of dogs.

Gizzy, as we most often called her, apparently wasn't too fond of the new arrangements or of living with all those dogs. She didn't stay long before she came up missing. However, about a week later she showed up back at my son's house looking for 'The Master.' It took time and considerable effort but gradually we were able to convince her that we were trustworthy and she would eventually become comfortable enough to adopt us.

This story is about her life and the experiences she might have had during her travels from a strange, far-away land back to her old neighborhood where, instead of The Master, she found a friendly Old Guy and Old Gal whom she would slowly learn to love.

ADVENTURES OF GIZZY

Chapter 1

Gizzy's Early Years

She was born on a rainy morning several hours before the sun came up. A tiny white and grey ball of fluff, she was the 3rd in a litter of 5 kittens with two brothers and two sisters whom she grew to love more than anything in her world.

Gizzy is the kitty in the middle

She loved her mom too and from the very beginning she could tell that her mom loved her. She would never get to know her dad, Mom never talked about him and it seemed to be the way things would always be.

Dinner time

She had begun life, living under a pile of boards and junk in the backyard of *The Master*.

Gizzy's birthplace

A couple of her aunts visited from time to time, but she never really got to know them. They weren't very friendly anyway and in reality, she was kind of afraid of them.

Gizzy's two mean aunts

They were not nice to her, like her mom and her brothers and sisters always were. She was just a kitten, but she was already beginning to form her own ideas about what she liked and didn't like quite so much.

After a while, The Master began to call her Gizzy and sometimes she was called Gizmo. She liked Gizzy better and decided that she really liked The Master, but especially when he rubbed her head or scratched her back. He was very gentle with her and she was just certain that she was his favorite.

Gizzy's two brothers

As Gizzy grew there came a day when she realized that her two brothers were no longer around. She wondered about that, but never fully understood why. She tried to talk to her mom about it, but Mom wasn't certain what had happened to them. Mom told her that things like that sometimes happen in a cat's life, but she assured Gizzy that they had a nice new home. She couldn't explain it, but it was something that humans thought was best and so she guessed that would always be the way of things.

Gizzy with her two sisters a few days after birth

Then one day both of her sisters disappeared and it was only Gizzy, her mom and the one scary aunt whom she had learned was named Sky. The mean and crazy old aunt had also gone missing and again Mom didn't seem to know why or where she had gone. Gizzy wasn't as sad about the mean aunt being gone as she was about her brothers and sisters. She really missed them and she missed all the fun they always had playing together.

Sometimes there was a girl who lived with The Master. She had heard The Master call the girl Christy and heard the girl call The Master Daddy.

Gizzy liked Christy because she had always been real nice and friendly to her. The only problem was that Christy sounded so much like Gizzy that sometimes when The Master called out a name they both thought he was saying their name and they would both come. Every time Christy saw Gizzy she would feed her treats and scratch her head. Gizzy really liked having her head scratched, but she liked getting the treats even better.

Gizzy wanted to ask Christy what had happened to the rest of her family, but she had never been able to make Christy understand what she was trying to say. It always seemed like they were each speaking a different language.

Besides, Christy had always seemed to like the dog better than Gizzy or her family members. She always seemed to pay much more attention to him. She called him Chaz and she seemed to speak to him quite often. Gizzy didn't understand what they were saying and it didn't seem to her that Chaz spoke the same language as Christy, but for some reason it seemed like they both understood each other better than Gizzy understood either of them. Chaz always seemed to be friendly to everyone, including Gizzy. He was just a real goofy, friendly guy, but sometimes other dogs would visit and Chaz wasn't always friendly with them. As a matter of fact, those other dogs didn't seem to want to be friendly with anybody including Gizzy and her mom.

Christy, Chaz and The Master

Whenever anyone new came to the house Chaz always acted like he knew them and always jumped up and put his front paws on them. Gizzy just didn't understand how a dog could possibly know everybody who came to the house when she didn't feel like she knew any of them. Maybe dogs are a lot smarter than cats. She didn't really believe that, but she made a vow to herself that one day she would find out.

By now Gizzy and her mom had moved into the big house with The Master.

Much of the time there were other people around. Gizzy noticed that when these other people were around, there was something that they called music which was always real loud and they all seemed to talk really loud. It seemed like they were trying to talk louder than the music. Then someone would make the music get even louder which would make everybody talk even louder. It seemed to Gizzy that if they didn't make the music so loud, they wouldn't have to talk so loud, but nobody seemed to care what Gizzy thought.

Sometimes they would turn off the music and they would all sit around and look at a big box with flashing colored lights on the front of it. Every once in a while The Master would jump up and start yelling and slapping his hands together. Sometimes the others would do that too, but not always at the same time as The Master. It seemed like they didn't like the same bright lights as The Master did.

After watching these strange things happen for quite a while, Gizzy figured out that they only did these strange things when something they called "football" was on the big box. She had no idea what football was, but whatever it was it sure made The Master mad sometimes. Then again, there were other times when it made The Master really happy. Gizzy didn't understand how something could be so bad one time and so good at other times. She decided she still had a lot to learn.

The big box with the colored lights

Eventually things would quiet back down and the strangers would leave. Time would pass and then the strangers would come back. Not always the same strangers, but Gizzy noticed that they always seemed to play the music loud and when the music wasn't playing, the big box with the flashing colored lights was. Sometimes they both played at the same time and when that happened it was really, really loud. It seemed like almost always when the big box was playing the strangers and The Master seemed to be sitting around staring at it, but there were times when it played and nobody seemed to pay any attention to it. This was real confusing to Gizzy.

She didn't understand very many human words, but they seemed to have named the big box TV. She was not even a year old when she first decided that TV was nicer than music because TV didn't make as much noise and wasn't as loud as music.

Gizzy also noticed that when all the strangers showed up The Master didn't seem to have time to scratch her head or pet her. As a matter of fact he didn't pay any attention to her at all. She decided that she didn't like these strangers and wasn't going to be friendly to them. She had never really quite understood what was so interesting about that big box, but she decided she didn't like it very much either.

ADVENTURES OF GIZZY

Chapter 2

Gizzy's Favorite Places

Over the next few months Gizzy discovered many favorite places where she liked to lay. Some places were better for sleeping and some were better for watching and at different times of the day, those special places would change.

In the morning, she had a favorite place where the sun would always be shining and she could lay there for a long time in the warmth created by the sun.

After a while the sun wouldn't be on her place and she'd change to a place where she could see out the window and watch the big dog that lived next door.

Sometimes her mom would sit with her and they would both look out the window.

Sometimes the squirrel that lived in the big tree across the street would come to tease the big dog.

Gizzy liked to watch when that happened and secretly began to like the squirrel. She wished that she could be as brave as that squirrel was. It never let that big dog scare it and seemed to take a lot of joy out of teasing him. For some reason Gizzy really enjoyed the days when that big dog would go nuts chasing the squirrel.

She wasn't real sure, but she thought maybe that squirrel had a brother or a sister or maybe a friend because sometimes she was certain she saw more than one of them and they didn't all seem to be the same color.

Gizzy also had a place in the back room where the sun would shine in the afternoon and she had a place way, way out in the junk room where she could get up real high and it was always a lot quieter.

Gizzy couldn't count, cause her mom had never taught her how, but she knew that she had a lot of good places to hide. In her mind, numbers didn't matter and she didn't care what number it was. Life was good and she really liked her life, but still she missed her sisters and brothers.

Gizzy was bothered by the fact that The Master and Christy didn't seem to miss them. In fact, Gizzy couldn't remember if they had even given her brothers and sisters names. If they had, Gizzy had never heard them mentioned.

She had secret names that she remembered them by, but she had never heard her mom, Christy or The Master call any of them by name. She thought that was strange, but she knew she still had a lot to learn about the ways of the human world.

ADVENTURES OF GIZZY
Chapter 3
Learning to Hunt

As time went on Gizzy's mom taught her how to sneak up on things. Mom would sometimes crouch down and stay perfectly still for a long, long time.

Then she would suddenly spring at whatever it was that she had been watching.

It might be a lizard

or maybe a frog,

sometimes it would be a grasshopper

or even more often it would be a mouse

Gizzy's mom was really good at catching things and sometimes after she caught something she and Gizzy would play with it. They would let it lay there for a while and then when it tried to escape Mom would catch it again.

Sometimes Mom would let Gizzy catch something. It was a lot of fun, but at the same time she was teaching Gizzy how to hunt and survive on her own. She wanted her to learn how to hunt all by herself.

Even though The Master always seemed to keep their dish full of food and always seemed to keep a bowl of water near the food, Mom said that it was important for Gizzy to learn how to catch things.

Mom said that one day Gizzy might find herself all alone. She said, "I won't always be with you. Someday you will be on your own." She said these were lessons that would help Gizzy for the rest of her life. Rather than just play with these things, Mom would often eat them and she even had Gizzy eat some of them.

Gizzy really liked the taste of grasshopper,

but she wasn't too fond of the taste of frog.

Mouse and lizard tasted about the same and she could take it or leave it.

One time Mom had even snuck up on a bird and caught it.

Gizzy decided that she really liked bird meat, it was very tasty, but she didn't like any of them as much as the food that The Master always kept in their food dish.

Gizzy's food and water dishes

ADVENTURES OF GIZZY
Chapter 4
A New Home For Gizzy

One night The Master left with one of the strangers and Gizzy never saw him again. After a few days Christy, The Master's daughter, came and took Gizzy away to a different city and a different home.

Immediately she knew that she didn't like this new place. Nothing about it was familiar, except that the big dog was there, the one that The Master always seemed to like so much better than Gizzy did.

Gizzy's mom was not there and neither was The Master, but along with that big dog called Chaz there were two or three other dogs and they seemed to have the run of the place. No one ever scolded them and they seemed to be able to do anything they wanted without ever getting punished. Gizzy was used to being punished when she did things that The Master didn't like, but this was a whole different set up. It seemed like all of them played with each other, but none of them wanted to play with Gizzy. She was living all alone with a house full of strangers. Christy had brought her here in a box with no windows to see out. She had been real scared in the box, but when Christy let her out of it they were in this strange new place.... with all these strange, scary, unfriendly dogs.

She didn't like it. She didn't like it one bit and she knew from the very beginning that the first chance she got, she was going to escape and try to find her way back home where her mom and The Master lived.

Days passed slowly. It seemed like she had been in this new place for a long time, but it was really only several days. Of course Gizzy still couldn't count so it could have been a month for all she would know.

She didn't know exactly what she was going to do, but she knew she didn't want to stay in this place with all those dogs getting all the attention.

Even Christy, whom she had always thought was her friend, didn't seem to like her as much as she liked that big dog, Chaz. Christy hadn't even scratched her head since they had been here. In fact, she had hardly ever been around.

Gizzy didn't know where Christy had been, but every time she saw her she looked like she had been crying and she just wasn't friendly anymore. No treats, no petting, no head scratches. She was just being ignored by everyone in this new house,,,,, except the dogs and they weren't friendly at all. They growled at her and chased her.

Gizzy didn't understand human emotions, but Christy was mourning the death of her father (The Master) and that was why she wasn't as friendly lately. She would get better soon.

The dogs wouldn't let Gizzy get near the food dish and even when they didn't bother her, there was never any food in the dish. Well, at least not what she considered food. This stuff was way different than what The Master had always fed her and it smelled awful…. kinda like dog breath. Gizzy was very, very sad.

She was also very lonely because she was the only cat in the entire house. She missed The Master and she missed Mom. She even kinda missed crabby old Aunt Sky.

There was one younger guy she thought she could be friends with, but it wasn't worth hanging around to find out, so she vowed to herself that when she got her chance to escape she would take it.

There was another dog that tried to be friendly, but the other dogs laughed at him

and he quit trying to be friendly cause he didn't like being laughed at
.

Finally there came a day when they let her outside. She didn't know if she would ever get another chance like this, so as soon as she was alone she took off on a dead run.

Although Gizzy was really happy to be free, it's a big scary world for a cat who had never been alone this far from home. In fact, she had never been completely alone in her life. In the beginning she always had her brothers and sisters and, of course, her mom.

She also had always been around The Master and whenever strange dogs came around, he always protected her from them. Sometimes he'd let her go outside so she could keep away from them, but he also made her a bed up in a high area where only she and Mom had been able to get to it.

She had always been very thankful that The Master liked her so much that he made this special place for her and she just knew if she could ever find her way back to that place, The Master would take good care of her. She was determined that she would find her way back there and she would snuggle up to The Master to make sure he knew how much she loved and trusted him.

ADVENTURES OF GIZZY
Chapter 5
Gizzy on Her Own

Gizzy spent the first night after she escaped in the same neighborhood as the house from which she had just left. She could hear them calling for her, but she wouldn't come out of her hiding place.

During the night she hunted for some food and made her way into the next neighborhood. She got chased by some scary dogs and decided that the people in that neighborhood were very unfriendly. They even yelled at her and threw things.

She was very anxious to try to find her way back to where The Master lived. She wasn't really sure how she was going to do it, but it seemed like she had a feeling *(instinct)* as to which direction she needed to go. She wasn't very good at knowing distances either, but she had another *instinct* that it was a long trip. She wasn't sure she could do it, but it just had to be better than staying in this place where everybody seemed to be unfriendly. She really missed her mom and she was surprised at how much she missed The Master.

The next day she started off trying to find her way home. Using her instincts, she headed off in the direction she felt was right. For some unexplained reason she just seemed to know which way to go although this wasn't something she remembered her Mom having taught her; it just seemed to come natural to her. Even though it was strange to her, she liked these new feelings. She was suddenly confident that she would find her way home.

That night she found a dish full of food near a house. It smelled like dogs breath, but there didn't seem to be any dogs around so she ate her fill and moved on.

After traveling just a little ways further, she decided she was getting kind of tired so she climed up into a tree to take a little nap.

When she woke up it was daylight again. She wasn't really sure if she should travel during the daylight because she didn't want take any chances that Christy might find her and take her back to that bad house.

Although she could see real well in the dark, she had come to realize that humans didn't see so good in the dark. They always made it brighter after it got dark and Gizzy just had a feeling that it meant that they couldn't see as well in the dark.

For that reason she decided to do most of her traveling at night so there would be less of a chance of being spotted before she got where she was going. She spent most of the day in that tree just watching and observing things.

When it got dark she climbed down and started on her journey. She hadn't eaten anything all day so before she left, she checked that dish that smelled like dog breath again. It had some fresh food in it so she ate her fill and then she headed out.

That night she came to a big wide body of water. She was a little afraid of water and she wasn't sure if she could swim well enough to get to the other side. She also didn't know what kind of creatures might live in this water. Whatever they were, she had an instinct it might be better to try to find a way around it rather than take a chance on swimming it. She had no idea which direction she should go but her instincts were telling her to go to the right. So she did and before she had traveled very far she came to a road.
Gizzy knew about roads because her mom had taught her about them. Mom had always warned Gizzy that roads can be really, really dangerous. Gizzy's mom had taught her that

it wasn't the road that was dangerous; it was the cars and trucks. Roads are there for cars and trucks and you don't very often see a road that doesn't have a car or truck that will go whizzing by every once-in-a-while. Some roads will have a lot more cars and trucks than others and on some roads the cars and trucks go a lot faster than they do on others. The road near the house that Gizzy had grown up in was in a neighborhood with lots of houses and the cars and trucks didn't go real fast. Gizzy didn't know if this road was one where they went really fast or not, but she didn't want to take a chance on getting caught in the middle of the road when a car or truck came by until she had figured out just how fast they would be coming.

She decided to find a safe place and watch for a while until she had a better idea about what kind of road this was. It didn't take very long until there were lots and lots of cars and trucks whizzing by on this road. Gizzy was glad she had decided to wait because this was one of those roads where the cars and trucks went really fast. Gizzy decided to stay off of the road and travel in the area beside it.

She decided that she still had a lot of nighttime left and that it was still safe to travel so she came out of her safe place and resumed her journey. It wasn't long until she came to a bridge that went over the big body of water.

She was going to have to cross that bridge, but again she was going to have to trust her instincts. For some reason she had an instinctive feeling that it would be safe because there was a path beside the road and that path also went over the bridge. She thought maybe if she stayed on that path she wouldn't have to worry about the cars and trucks getting near her.

She watched for a while and determined that the cars and trucks didn't get near the path. She decided that it was safe to cross the bridge as long as she stayed on the path and didn't get out into the road. She made a run for it and as it turned out not one single car came by while she was crossing the bridge. She decided that it was good that she had followed her instincts and made up her mind that whenever she was faced with a big decision in the future she would always follow her instincts.

After traveling further Gizzy could tell that it was starting to become daylight. She had been traveling all night and she was getting pretty tired. She decided to see if she could find something to eat and a place to spend the day resting up. Just before daylight she found a dead bird lying beside the road.

Gizzy thought maybe the bird hadn't been careful about watching for cars and trucks. It was still warm, so she decided that it would be safe for her to eat it and she carried it to a nearby tree and climbed up into the tree to a safe place where she could eat while she watched things until she went to sleep!

She had been traveling all night and suddenly realized how tired she was. She went right to sleep and slept nearly the whole day away. Of course, she didn't sleep real soundly because she had to be aware of her surroundings. She was completely on her own and didn't have The Master to look after her. She had to be really, really careful all the time, now that she was alone.

She dozed until the late afternoon and then finished off the rest of the bird that she had found that morning. With a full stomach and all rested up like she was, she felt like she was ready for another night of traveling.

She got started before it became fully dark, but things didn't go as well as planned. After she had traveled only a short distance, she came to a big swamp.

She had spent a lot of time in the out-of-doors since the day she had been born, but she had never encountered anything quite like this. She ventured a short distance into the swamp and discovered that there was a lot of water in it. From all the different odors, she could tell that a lot of different creatures had spent time in this area. Some of the scents were smells that she was familiar with, but there were quite a few that she had never smelled before. She could smell lizards and frogs mostly, but there was a rabbit scent

and even squirrel scents.

She was pretty sure that she smelled a duck smell and she was pretty sure that it was a whole flock of ducks that she was smelling.

There was one smell that she was pretty sure was a snake smell….

…. And another that she was really certain was a turtle smell.

There was another that she couldn't identify, but it reminded her of an alligator smell that her mother had described to her and warned her about.

Her mom had taught her that snakes and alligators are both to be avoided when at all possible. Although you can always climb a tree to get away from them, some snakes can climb trees too. Besides why should she take the chance? She was on an adventure, but she didn't want to take unnecessary chances when she could avoid them.

She decided that she should probably not try to find her way through the swamp, but should instead try to find a way around it. Again, she relied on her instinct to tell her which way to go and again she decided to go to the right.

There was a road going in that direction, but again she wasn't sure how fast the cars and trucks might be on this road. She decided that it would be safer for her to travel in the high grassy areas beside the road rather than to stay on the road. She was sure that this would be slower, but she believed that it would be a whole lot safer. In this strange new world she didn't want to take any unnecessary chances.

She traveled the rest of that night and still hadn't found a way to get around the swamp. Since it was getting close to morning and she was getting really tired she decided that it might be time to look for a place to spend the day. She didn't see any houses, so she didn't think she would be finding any dog food to fill up on.

She had watched her mom catch lizards and birds ever since she was a baby kitten and her mom had insisted that she learn how to do it too, so she was pretty sure she could find something to eat.

She decided to find a good place to spend the day and then to watch for a chance to catch herself a meal. As luck would have it, shortly after the sun came up she was able to catch herself a frog. It wasn't her favorite food, but it would do for today.

She made herself a promise that tomorrow she would find a house where she could get some decent dog food. It was not that dog food was her favorite, but she did like it so much better than frog.

ADVENTURES OF GIZZY
Chapter 6
Home at Last

Finally after all the nights of traveling, Gizzy came to the neighborhood where she was born. She still had a ways to travel to get back to The Master's house, but there were a lot of familiar things that she recognized in this neighborhood. Mom used to take her on journeys around the old neighborhood when she was teaching her to hunt.

She knew that she was getting close to home and by this time tomorrow night she would be back there. She would sleep much better tonight, knowing that she was back in familiar territory. She found a familiar yard, where she knew she would be able to find food in the morning. She crawled under a familiar pile of lumber where she had hidden several times in the past. She knew there was an unfriendly dog that lived in this house, but there were also a couple of cats that she knew from earlier times and she felt certain they would share some of their food with her in the morning.

For the first time in a long time she slept during the night instead of during the daytime. She slept really well that night and awoke feeling refreshed and excited to be so close to her home. It was really nice to be in familiar territory.

The next morning she checked on the food situation and just as she had suspected, there was a dish of fresh cat food in the same place it had always been. She ate just enough to take the hunger pains away because she didn't want to eat all of the food that her old friends were expecting to be there for them.

Being in familiar territory made her feel safe traveling in the day light and she set out to make the rest of her journey home. She knew all the short cuts from here to The Master's house. She knew that she would eat her next meal in her own yard. Well, at least in the yard that used to be hers. She didn't really know why The Master had never come back or why she had been hauled away to that strange house with all the dogs. There were a lot of unknowns that she still had to get figured out, but she was happy to be back in familiar territory and those things could wait until she got home.

She arrived at The Master's home when the sun was straight up overhead. She knew that it was the middle of the day and that it was the hottest part of the day and she wanted to find a cool place to lie down and rest and to study things. She spent the rest of the day on the roof of the friendly Old Guy who lived next door to The Master's house. There was a tree right beside of the house and it had always been easy for Gizzy to climb that tree and get out onto the roof. There was lots of shade where that tree hung over the roof. It gave her a nice cool place where she could observe everything without being seen. She spent the rest of the daylight hours just watching and studying things. She was hopeful that The Master would have returned by now, but The Master's house appeared to be silent and empty. It was obvious that neither The Master nor her mom were anywhere to be found.

She was glad that the friendly Old Guy still lived here. He reminded her so much of The Master and she had always liked him.

Unfortunately, he never seemed very anxious to feed her and she was very hungry. She wanted to get close to him to see if he might feed her, but she was afraid he might try to trap her and make her go back to that house with all the dogs in it. She decided to let him see her, but she would stay her distance to make sure he didn't try to capture her. She waited until he was sitting in a chair on the patio and then she came down off the roof and made sure he saw her. He didn't seem to be surprised to see her and he mumbled some words to her. He had a gruff voice and she wasn't sure if he was saying nice things or nasty things. Pretty soon he got up and went into the house. He left the door open, but Gizzy had never been in his house and she wasn't about to go in there now. He was only in the house for a few minutes when he came back out and put a bowl of food and a bowl of water out where Gizzy could get to it. She still didn't trust him so she didn't go right to the food even though she was really very hungry.

She waited around and kept an eye on him. He went and sat back down and pretty soon the Old Gal that lived with him came out and sat down with him.

Gizzy had always liked the Old Gal even though she had never offered to pet her. They sat there for a while drinking something and then they got up and went into the house. As soon as they left she started eating some of the food and took a drink of the water. She didn't eat much of it because she didn't know for sure who it was intended for. It might be that the Old Guy had a cat of his own now. Or maybe it was for a dog. It didn't smell like dogs breath, but Gizzy had learned that sometimes things can be deceiving. She really didn't know if she could trust him not to capture her.

She ate a little that night and the next day she noticed that the dish was full again. The water was fresh too. That night she ate her fill and the next morning when she came back the bowl was full again.

After a few days passed she saw Christy again, but she wasn't real anxious to get close to her, cause she still remembered being trapped in that awful box with no windows and being taken to that awful house full of dogs. She knew if Christy got her hands on her she might try to take her back there again. She didn't want to go, but she knew that if that should happen she would be able to find her way back home again. She had done it once, and she was absolutely certain she could do it again.

That made her feel like it might be safe to give Christy another chance. She didn't go right up to her, but she made sure that Christy saw her. She stayed away from her for a while and Christy didn't make any attempt to capture her again. She was beginning to think that things were going to be OK and maybe Christy wouldn't take her back to that bad place again after all.

The Old Guy having coffee

After watching them for a while Gizzy heard Christy call the Old Guy Grampy. That confused Gizzy for a few minutes because she had always thought of the Old Guy as a bit grumpy and Christy was calling him Grampy. In her mind she decided Grampy was a term of endearment to Christy and that she must really like the Old Guy. Gizzy started thinking that this just might work out after all.

As the days passed she began to get friendly with The Old Guy and the Old Gal who lived with him.

They seemed to want to be friendly too, but she just didn't trust humans anymore because of some of those encounters she had been through on the long journey back home from that bad house with the bad dogs.

Other than those few instances, she hadn't had very many bad experiences with strange humans. She had never gotten close with any of the humans who came to visit with The Master. None of them had ever seemed like they wanted her to be friendly with them, so she had always stayed her distance.

Each morning she would go to the area where the Old Guy was keeping the food dish and each time it would have fresh food in it. She hadn't seen any other cats, there weren't any dogs around and it didn't smell like dogs breath. She decided that the Old Guy intended this food for her and she began to feel that he was still her friend.

Finally she started allowing him to see her eat out of his dish every so often and he didn't seem to mind. He started leaving the door of his house open and each day the food dish would be closer to the door. Then one day the dish was just inside of the door. Gizzy was sort of afraid to go into the house to eat. She was afraid that the Old Guy might try to trap her. He hadn't seemed to want to do her any harm, but she was still leery. She decided to chance it and she stepped into the house to eat. She ate fast and went right back outside as soon as she had eaten.

The next day the food dish was a little further in the house, but again Gizzy ate and left right away. After a few days the food dish was on a paper and there was a water dish beside of it. Gizzy studied this and remembered that this was the way things had always been at The Master's house. She decided that the Old Guy wanted to be her friend and that she should give him a chance. She saw him sitting in a chair and he was looking at one of those big boxes that humans call a TV. He didn't seem to be paying any attention to her so she decided to explore a little bit. She snuck behind a big piece of furniture and came out on the other end of it.

From there she could see into another room and there didn't seem to be any danger so she ventured into it to look around. She didn't want to get caught in here, so she decided to retrace her footsteps and get back outside. Maybe tomorrow, if things didn't change, she would explore a little more.

This went on for several days and Gizzy was getting quite comfortable in this new house. There weren't any dogs here. That was one really good thing about it. Another was that the Old Guy and the Old Gal had both tried to be friendly to her. She wasn't about to get too comfortable with them, but she was beginning to relax a little more each time she went into the house. It even got to the point where she started finding comfortable places to spend a little time lying in the sunny spots and watching out the windows. She was able to come and go any time she wanted and there was always fresh food and water in the dishes. And best of all it didn't smell like dogs breath.

One day when Gizzy was lying in her favorite sunny spot, she heard the door close. This really made her nervous. She immediately got up and went to the door and sure enough it was closed. She was trapped! How could she have been so foolish as to trust this Old Guy? He'd probably put her in one of those boxes with no windows and take her back to that house with all the dogs.

She didn't know just what to do, but she began to meow. She meowed several times and she noticed the Old Guy coming toward her. She decided to stand her ground and if he tried to pick her up she was going to scratch him. To her surprise, he didn't try to pick her up, all he did was open the door and mumble some words to her. She didn't wait around to see anything else, she just bolted out the door and headed for the nearest tree. She hurried up the tree and found a good place to watch things. To her surprise, the Old Guy just closed the door and she didn't hear anything else. She stayed in the tree for quite a long time.

She spent that night hunting and watching and observing things, but when morning came she went to the door and waited. Sure enough, after a little while the Old Guy came to the door and picked up his newspaper. He saw Gizzy sitting there and mumbled something to her. She still didn't understand very many human words, but he seemed to be friendly and he seemed to be holding the door open for her.

She was very reluctant, but she remembered that all she had to do was meow a couple times the day before and he came and opened the door for her. She decided that he didn't mean her any harm and that he was trying his very best to be friendly. So, she jumped up on the stoop and went into the house. Sure enough there was fresh food and fresh water in the dishes. The Old Guy closed the door and went about his business. He sat at the table and seemed to be looking at the newspaper, but most importantly, he wasn't paying any attention to Gizzy.

She ate a little and got herself a drink of water then she sat by the door and watched the Old Guy. He looked over at her and mumbled a few words. Gizzy had no idea what he was saying, but she turned and looked at the door and stood up. That got the Old Guy to stand up and he came over and opened the door and Gizzy slipped outside. She turned around and sat down just outside the door and the Old Guy just stood there and looked at her. He held the door open and seemed to be trying to get her to come back in. Well, she really had been enjoying that sunny place in the front window and he had opened the door as soon as he saw her sitting by it. She decided to go back in and lay in the sun for a while.

For the next few days Gizzy showed up in the morning and waited by the door until the Old Guy came to get his paper. He would hold the door open and she would go in, have a few bites of food, drink some water and go on about her business. The Old Guy and the Old Gal did pretty much the same.

Gizzy had figured out that she could get them to do pretty much whatever she wanted them to do. All she had to do was stand by the door and wait until they noticed her and they would let her out. Sometimes if they didn't notice her, she would meow and they would come let her out. Gizzy was pretty sure this was going to be her new home for a long time. She decided she would try to be friendlier with these people and she would watch after them as best she could.

One thing that Gizzy was really grateful for was that the Old Guy didn't have one of those chairs that had hurt her. When she had lived with The Master he had a chair that had pinched her tail. Her tail had never been right after that and it always had a bend in the end of it. Ever since that day she had been forever fearful of that chair which she had come to know was a *rocking chair*.

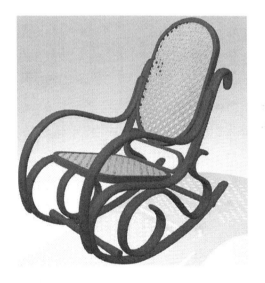

Weeks passed and she was becoming more and more comfortable. She would let them scratch her head and pet her, but she wasn't going to start purring and let them know that she was enjoying this treatment.

She would lie down beside them, but she wasn't about to get into their lap, but after this had gone on for quite a long time she decided she would see what happened if she did get up into the Old Gal's lap. She laid beside her for a while and let her pet her and scratch her head. Then after a while she crawled up into the Old Gal's lap. As she continued to pet her and scratch her head she started having memories of The Master. She decided that these humans were doing the best that they could at taking his place and she began to believe that this was what true happiness is all about.

Then one day when Gizzy showed up at the door, the Old Guy didn't come to get his paper. In fact there wasn't any paper there. Gizzy wondered about it, but she decided that he would come let her in later. She waited around by the door for quite a long time, but he never came. After a while Christy came driving into the driveway. She opened the door and got some food and water and sat it outside where Gizzy could get to it. She didn't stay very long before she left again.

The next day the same thing happened again. No paper, no Old Guy, no food and no water, then Christy comes again. After this happened for quite a few days a different Old Guy stopped and put food and water in her dishes. The next day Christy was back. It seemed to Gizzy that the Old Guy and Old Gal had come up missing just like The Master had way back when. The only good thing about it was that she was beginning to think that all strangers aren't as nasty as the ones she ran into on her way back from that strange house where all those dogs had been. The one that Christy had taken her to after The Master had left her alone in the old house next door.

After quite a long time, just as Gizzy was thinking that they might never come back, the Old Guy and the Old Gal did come back. They drove their car in and parked it in the same place that they had always parked it.

When they got out of the car they were both dragging some kind of a big colorful box. They dragged them all the way into the house. Gizzy had never seen anything like it before. She got real curious about those pretty boxes and tried to pay real close attention to what they were going to do with them. She followed them into the bedroom and they put those big boxes up on the bed. Pretty soon Gizzy heard a strange sound. It was kinda like zzzzzzippppp.

She paid real close attention and the Old Guy and the Old Gal began to take things out of those big boxes. They hung them up in the little room and put some of them in the big wooden box that always sits beside the bed. After a while, the pretty boxes were closed up and Gizzy heard that zzzzzzzippppp sound again.

Then the pretty boxes were taken off of the bed and put in the little room where they had hung all the clothes. Gizzy thought she heard someone call that room a closet and she thought someone had called the pretty boxes suitcases. The Old Guy had called the big box that sat beside the bed a dresser. Of course her knowledge of human language was still very limited, but she was learning more all the time. One day maybe she would be able to talk to them like she used to be able to talk to her mom.

ADVENTURES OF GIZZY
Chapter 7
Settling into a New Home

For the next few days things seemed to be back to normal. Each morning Gizzy would wait by the door until the Old Guy came to get his newspaper. He would let her in and she would eat a good meal, then she would find a nice place to lie down and let her breakfast settle. She would sleep for a while and enjoy the sunny place in the window where he had made her a bed.

In the afternoon the Old Gal would settle in to watch the big box with the colored lights and Gizzy would often lie down beside her while she watched it. The Old Gal would sometimes scratch Gizzy's head and she almost forgot herself and started to purr. She realized that she was really starting to trust this Old Gal and was really starting to enjoy spending time in this new house. She still wasn't ready to purr for these people, but she was willing to give them a chance to prove that they could be good friends.

Then one day a new lady came to visit. She had a big dog with her and Gizzy really didn't think she was going to like this new lady. She definitely didn't like that big dog. He seemed to want to be friendly, but he was so big and so muscular that Gizzy just knew that he would never be a good friend. Of course that probably didn't matter much because she had never been real friendly with any dog except when she had first gotten to know Christy's dog, Chaz.

The lady had started right in talking in a friendly tone and trying to make friends with Gizzy and even though she had that big dog smell about her, she seemed to be nice. Gizzy paid real close attention and after a while she figured out that the big dog's name was Leha and that the lady was called

Heather. After more time passed she heard Heather call the Old Gal Mom. That made Gizzy feel good to know that she was part of the family and it reminded her again just how much she missed her own mom. Gizzy decided she would see how things played out and would allow Heather a chance to be friendly, but she didn't have the same thoughts about Leha.

Heather and Leha

After a short time Heather sat down and seemed to be motioning for Gizzy to sit beside her. Well, she decided this was the best time to see just how friendly they were going to be. She jumped up beside Heather, who then reached out and started scratching her head.

Gizzy waiting for Heather to scratch her head.

Nobody had to tell Gizzy twice to let her head be scratched. When it came to humans, it was her most favorite thing ever. They just seemed to be built perfectly for expert head scratching. Gizzy made up her mind right then and there that Heather would be a friend as long as she was inclined to scratch her head. She hoped that Heather would move in and stay with the Old Gal forever.

Things didn't turn out that way, but Heather did visit quite often and she always remembered to scratch Gizzy's head for a while. Gizzy liked it so much that she forgot her rule about not purring and found herself purring for Heather quite often. She felt that if Heather heard her purr she would know just how much she enjoyed having her head scratched and so far it seemed to be working out quite well.

Gizzy enjoying her new yard and surroundings

Gizzy decided that life is good and there are a lot of good humans, maybe even more good ones than those mean ones she had run into on the long journey home from that strange place where Christy had taken her all those weeks ago. Gizzy was really happy with her new home and her new friends.

ADVENTURES OF GIZZY
Chapter 8
Gizzy's Fears

Gizzy had been living in the new house with the Old Folks for quite some time now, but she still hadn't gotten over some of her old fears. Everytime someone would come and knock on the door, no matter what Gizzy was doing, she would run and hide behind the biggest thing in the house. It was that long soft bench that Heather had sat on when she scratched Gizzy's head. It always sat next to the wall and it was a perfect hiding place. She knew that she'd be safe back there and she always stayed there for a long time or until she knew it was safe to come out. Sometimes the doorbell would ring and Gizzy would be off to her hiding place. Whenever someone strange would come into the house,

Gizzy would hide. She didn't trust humans and it took a long time for anyone new to earn her trust. Some of them talked with a real gruff voice. Those humans she would never allow herself to trust. Some of them talked in a friendly voice like the voice Heather used when she talked to Gizzy.

One day two of those humans came to visit. Gizzy had hidden as soon as they came through the door, but she was curious. She could smell a cat smell on one of these girls and that made her really curious. She hadn't smelled other cat smells in this house in all the time she had been coming here. She wanted to find out more about these new humans. She paid real close attention and she noticed that the Old Guy and the Old Gal seemed to like them a lot. They talked with them for quite a while and it seemed to Gizzy that their names were Rachel and Kylie. Gizzy seemed to feel that their voices were familiar and when they got closer, she could tell that they really did have a cat smell about them.

As Gizzy tried to go back in her memory and tried to remember back to the days when she had lived with The Master it seemed to her that she remembered Rachel coming to visit. That's it! She thought, I remember Rachel used to treat me really nice when she came to visit Christy.

She tried real hard and she thought she could remember Kylie coming to visit too.

With those thoughts in her mind, she came out from her hiding spot and jumped right up beside Rachel on the big soft bench. She snuggled up close to her and hoped that Rachel would remember her. It was working. Rachel got real giddy and squealed the same squeal that Gizzy remembered from all the times she had visited Christy in The Masters house. Gizzy was just certain that she had heard Rachel call her Gizmo when she was talking to Kylie. Almost nobody ever called her Gizmo these days. Everyone called her Gizzy. Though she liked Gizzy much better, it was comforting to hear Rachel call her Gizmo. It was like meeting an old friend, which is exactly what she considered both Rachel and Kylie to be.

Rachel and Kylie

Kylie began to scratch her head and rub her tummy and Gizzy was ever so happy that she had come out from her hiding place to see who had come to visit.

She was beginning to think that all of the things that scared her were not really all that bad and that maybe she should think about not hiding every time some sound frightened her. Then again, she just wasn't that brave and she knew that hiding is always safer than taking that chance. Besides, she could always hide first, then study the situation and if things didn't seem to be too bad she could come out after giving it some extra thought. That had worked out quite well with Rachel and Kylie. There was no reason to think it wouldn't work again. Besides, some of those loud noises that scared her so much hadn't proven to be so friendly.

She remembered lots of times when those loud noises had come and then there were real bright flashes of light. No wait, that's not right, the flashes of light always came first, then the loud noise.

Gizzy remembered now. When she was still a kitten her mom had taught her that when you see that bright flash of light be prepared for a loud noise right after it.

For some reason Mom had always told Gizzy that the flash of light was much more dangerous than the loud bang that always followed it. Gizzy never did quite understand that, but Mom had always been very clear about it. The sound will scare you, but the light can hurt you real bad. That's what her mom had always said and that's exactly why

Gizzy always hid when she heard those loud noises. She was hiding from the bright lights, not the loud noises, but humans didn't seem to be smart enough to understand that. They always thought it was the noises when it was really the bright lights all along.

Whenever the bright flashes came the booms would come and most of the time when the booms came it would get really wet. Gizzy remembered that her mom had taught her the human words. The bright flashes were called lightning, the loud noises were called thunder and the wet that sometimes came with them was called rain.

Lightning was dangerous. The thunder, though scary sounding wasn't dangerous, but it was almost always accompanied by the danger of lightning. Most of the time if you had lightning you also had thunder, but sometimes it was so far away that you saw the lightning, but hardly even heard the thunder. Other times you would hear the thunder, but not notice the lightning. Then there were times when you had lightning and thunder you also were going to get wet if you didn't take cover because lightning and thunder often bring rain.

Sometimes Gizzy would hear other loud noises and she would hide thinking that the lightning might be coming too. When she would hear those loud noises they wouldn't be as loud as thunder and she eventually began to understand that they were different than thunder and lightning.

She didn't remember Mom ever telling her about these other sounds, but she knew that every so often they would come. She had learned from the Old Guy and the Old Gal that these other loud noises were called fireworks. Gizzy didn't like that word. Mom had told her one time about fire and that it was dangerous. She didn't know if fireworks had anything to do with fire, but they sounded a lot alike and it didn't sound safe to her. She didn't like the sound of it whether it was dangerous or not. She just knew that she wanted to hide whenever she heard them.

Sometimes the fireworks would sound like it was a long ways away and sometimes it would sound like it was right down the street. One time, when it sounded like it was right down the street, Gizzy had gotten brave after the sound had been going on for quite a long time and she got up the nerve to look out the window from her favorite bed. She had seen lots of bright lights that looked a lot like the colored lights she would see on the TV.

She hadn't been afraid of the TV for a long time now and she was beginning to think that these fireworks might not be all that dangerous.

Then again, why take a chance? So, Gizzy decided she would always hide whenever she heard fireworks.

ADVENTURES OF GIZZY
Chapter 9
A New Feeder

As time passed, Gizzy became more and more comfortable living with the Old Folks. She didn't spend the nights living in the house, she always went out when the Old Guy or the Old Gal would indicate it was time to go out, but she would always be allowed back in the next morning. Whenever she came in there would be fresh food and water waiting for her.

Then one day when she came in there was this big strange looking dish with her food inside it, but no way to get into it. The dish didn't seem to have any opening. Well, the only opening it had was way too small for Gizzy to get to the food. She was confused.

How in the world was she supposed to eat her breakfast? She sat beside the big dish and was pondering what she should do next when she heard a whirrrring sound and food came sliding down the chute and landed in the little tray that Gizzy had been trying to get into. She checked and this was definitely the same food that she had been eating for weeks. She didn't understand what had just happened, but she decided to give it a chance and see how this strange new contraption worked. Maybe all she had to do was stick her paw up that little hole than sit back and stare at the contraption. It had worked once and she decided that maybe that was the way this thing worked.

That afternoon, when she came in from a day of roaming around the neighborhood and went to her food spot there was food in the tray again. There was also fresh water in the water dish. Nice! Gizzy decided that she had done a real good job of training the Old Guy and the Old Gal how to care for a cat. She just knew that this was going to become her favorite home of all time.

Each morning when she came in she would stop by the food place. Sometimes the food would already be in the tray, but sometimes Gizzy would have to wait. She would get herself a drink of fresh water and then she would stick her paw up that little hole. Then she would sit by the food dish and stare at it waiting for that strange whirrrring sound. Whenever she heard that sound, food would come falling out and land in the tray. No matter where Gizzy was in the house when she heard that whirrrring sound she would come running and always there would be fresh food in the tray. Gizzy would eat and go on about the day. She'd sleep in the sun for a while, then she would go to the other window and watch that neighborhood dog for a while. This was the same dog she had always watched from The Master's window. Strange, she hadn't thought about The Master in quite some time. She wondered why he had never come back. She wished she understood humans better. Maybe then she would be able to ask about The Master and how he was doing. In the meantime, Gizzy was real happy with the way things had worked out. Later in the day she would lie beside the Old Gal again while she watched the colored lights on the big box. She'd get her head scratched for a while and she'd listen for that whirrring sound. Sometimes the food would just drop out by itself, without Gizzy sticking a paw up the hole. Whenever she would hear that whirrring sound she would know that dinner had been served.

As the weeks passed Gizzy began to put on weight. That new food dish always had food in it. She ate as much as she wanted anytime she wanted and as often as she wanted. She had settled in to a new lifestyle that didn't require her to hunt for her food and she was getting far more food than she ever had at any other time in her life. Those times when she did get the urge to hunt she would often bring the kill home and leave it for the Old Guy beside his newspaper. She wanted him to know how much she appreciated all that he did for her.

The combination of those two things, more food/less exercise were coming together to make her fat. The strange thing was she didn't care. She was happy and she had been training the Old Folks to attend to her needs. They were really smart humans and had learned well. She had begun to think that life was really, really good.

ADVENTURES OF GIZZY
Chapter 10
A New Flea Collar

One day the Old Gal and Heather came driving into the driveway and got out of the car with some packages in their arms. They went into the house and left the door open so that Gizzy could follow them in. Heather sat down and motioned for Gizzy to come sit beside her.

Well Gizzy had come to realize that this meant she was going to get a little head scratching and you never had to ask her twice if she would like her head scratched. She jumped up beside Heather and sprawled out on her back giving her both the head to scratch and the tummy to rub. Whichever one Heather decided to give her attention to would be just fine with Gizzy.

Heather did rub her tummy for a while and she talked to her some in that nice friendly voice that she used only when she was talking to Gizzy. Gizzy had noticed that she never talked in that nice voice when she talked to Leha and she didn't use that voice when she talked to the Old Gal. It was a voice she reserved only for Gizzy and Gizzy just loved it when she did.

Heather was talking with Gizzy and using that really nice voice but she was up to something and Gizzy wasn't sure just what. It seemed like she had something in her hand and she was trying to get Gizzy to smell of it. Gizzy did smell it and it didn't smell like anything she would want to eat. She was pretty sure it wasn't a treat, although Heather had often given her treats.

If it wasn't a treat, maybe it was a new toy. Heather had brought her toys before too. There was one toy that Gizzy really liked. It had a toy mouse on the end of a long stiff string and when the humans wanted Gizzy to play with it, it would go round and round in circles. Gizzy would jump on it and trap it just like her mom had taught her to do when she was a kitten and her mom was teaching her to hunt. Soon she found out that if she didn't hang on to it real tight it would take off again and start running around in a circle again. That reminded Gizzy of all the fun times she had enjoyed with her mom when she was teaching Gizzy to hunt for food. Gizzy liked remembering those old times.

It seemed like this toy mouse never got tired of running around in that circle. Gizzy could trap it as many times as she wanted and each time she let it loose it would start running around in the same circle. Gizzy would play with it for a while and then she'd get bored by it. She'd just lay back and watch it run around in the circle. Finally one of the humans would come over and touch it and it would stop running….. until the next time Gizzy started swatting at it…. Then one of the humans would touch it again and it would start all over again.

Gizzy liked this game and she played it a lot for quite a long time.

Then one night when she came into the house for dinner she noticed that the mouse game was gone. She never did find out just what happened to it, but she wondered if this new toy that Heather was having her smell was going to be as much fun as that mouse game had been.

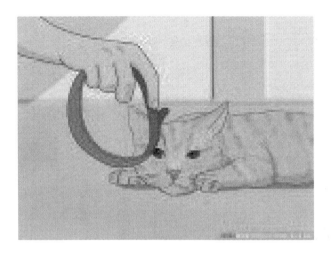

Heather was poking it at Gizzy and it seemed like she wanted her to put her nose into it. Well Heather had never done anything to disappoint Gizzy, so she had no reason to distrust her now. She did put her nose into the new game and the next thing you know Heather slipped it up over her head and tightened it around her neck. Gizzy didn't like this game and she pulled away and shook as hard as she could, but she couldn't get the toy off of her neck. She jumped down and shook her head from side to side and up and down, but the toy just wouldn't come off.

She couldn't believe that Heather meant her any harm and so she didn't think that this new game would hurt her, but it sure was going to take some time getting used to it.

For the next several days Gizzy tried over and over again to get that game off of her neck, but she just wasn't having any luck. Then one evening the Old Gal was scratching her head when she heard a loud "SNIP" sound. After that Gizzy noticed that the long part of the new game was gone. Now it was just a ring around her neck and it didn't bother her as much as it had when Heather had first put it on her. She listened closely when the Old Gal talked to her and she heard her call the new game by the name of "flea collar."

Gizzy still didn't know much about the human's language, but she had come to know that fleas were pesky little bugs and they like to bite. Gizzy had often encountered them when she was out an about and it seemed to her like they were all teeth. She didn't like them at all and if this flea collar thing would help to keep them away from her, she was all for it.

That was the end of that conversation and Gizzy wore that flea collar for a long time. Then one evening when the Old Gal was petting her she heard that loud "SNIP" sound again and she noticed that the flea collar fell off into the Old Gal's lap. Gizzy really felt free again and she got up and shook and scratched her neck.

It felt so good to be out of that collar and she rolled around and stretched and scratched her neck and just really felt free.

It had been a long time since she had felt this kind of freedom and she decided that she liked it better than wearing that thing around her neck.

Then she noticed the Old Gal coming toward her holding something out and offering her a smell of it.

Sure enough it was another flea collar. Gizzy decided she wasn't going to fall for that same old trap again and she pulled away.

She ran and hid behind the biggest thing in the house. It was that long soft bench that Heather always sat on when she scratched Gizzy's head. It always sat next to the wall and it was a perfect hiding place. She was pretty sure she had heard the Old Gal and the Old Guy call it a couch. Whatever it was called, she knew that she'd be safe back there and she stayed there for a long time.

Finally, when it was time to go out for the night, Gizzy came out and meowed at the door. She could tell that the Old Gal wasn't very happy with her, but she just wanted to go out for the night. She'd come back in tomorrow morning and she was sure the Old Gal would be happy again. She was always happiest in the morning when she saw Gizzy for the first time.

Gizzy didn't remember how long it had been since she had gotten out of that flea collar, but she noticed that she was being bothered by fleas again.

Maybe there was some good reason for that collar after all. She decided that the next time someone tried to put a flea collar on her she wouldn't put up such a fuss. She was beginning to think that these humans only did things that were good for her and she decided she should try really hard to learn to trust them more.

ADVENTURES OF GIZZY

Chapter 11

Crossing the Rainbow Bridge

As time went on Gizzy came to really love the Old Guy and the Old Gal. She knew that she had been very lucky to have been a part of their family for so many years. It had been a long time since she had made the journey from the house with all the unfriendly dogs that lived with Christy. She had come to trust these humans nearly as much as she had trusted The Master. And since she did trust them, she wasn't afraid when they would pick her up and hold her in their lap.

She had even come to really enjoy it when the Old Gal would let her lie on her tummy so that she could pet her with both hands. During those times the Old Gal would scratch her head and pet her back both at the same time. Sometimes Gizzy would roll over on her back and she could get her tummy rubbed while she was getting her head scratched.

These were the best of times and she would sometimes forget her rule about not purring. When she was really happy it was hard to not purr. Besides, she was convinced that the Old Guy and the Old Gal both loved her nearly as much as The Master had loved her. Because of that love she had come to the decision that she would purr for the Old Gal when she did things like that.

Gizzy still hadn't convinced herself that she should purr for the Old Guy because he still sounded really gruff sometimes when he talked to her, but the Old Gal never sounded gruff and always seemed happy when Gizzy would sit on her lap. That made Gizzy want to reward the Old Gal by purring for her and many evenings she would seek out the Old Gal just so she could sit in her lap and enjoy all of the attention. And she would purr and purr as long as the Old Gal kept petting and scratching.

As cat years go, Gizzy had gotten to be quite old. She still didn't know how to count, but she had heard the Old Gal talking with Heather one day and she heard her tell her that Gizzy was now 15 years old. Gizzy didn't know how old that was in cat years, but she did know that she had been feeling less perky in recent weeks.

Lately she didn't have much of an appetite and had been leaving the food in her dish. When the whirrrring sound would happen Gizzy didn't get nearly as excited anymore. Sometimes the food in her dish would get so full that it was nearly running over the top. Then the Old Gal would take some of it out and put it back inside the big bubble that held the food.

After this went on for a while, the Old Guy tried to get Gizzy to eat some really great smelling food that was really moist. It smelled like fish and Gizzy was sure that it was very tasty. She forced herself to eat a little bit of it and that seemed to make the Old Guy happy.

The next few days Gizzy forced herself to eat these special treats that the Old Guy always tried to hand feed her. Some of them smelled like tuna fish and some smelled like sardines. One night it smelled like chicken and another night like turkey. She knew he was trying really hard to get her to eat these great foods, but she just didn't have the appetite for it. She knew she was losing weight and she knew that he was concerned about it. She really wanted to please the Old Guy to let him know how happy he had made her all these years, but she also knew that her time was drawing near.

She knew that she was going to have to be leaving this place where the Old Guy and the Old Gal had worked so hard to earn her trust. It was that old thing called instinct again.

Gizzy didn't know why she knew it was her time, but somehow she just knew.

Years earlier Mom had explained about The Rainbow Bridge. She had told her that when you cross The Rainbow Bridge all of your old friends who crossed the bridge before you will be there waiting for you.

Gizzy had been slowing down, not hunting as much, and enjoying her new lazy life with the Old Folks. She had still been going out at night because she liked to feel the fresh air on her face and she liked to smell all the strange smells in the neighborhood. During the daytime she was mostly staying in and napping. She had been sleeping more and dreaming about Mom and The Master waiting for her at that Rainbow Bridge Mom had told her about.

Gizzy was thinking that someday soon she may want to walk across that bridge to The Master and Mom. She was anxious to see if her brothers and sisters would all be there. She wondered if her mean old Aunts would be there too. How many other faces would she recognize? She wondered if she would miss the Old Folks or if they would miss her. Her instinct told her that everything would be ok. She would be with past loved ones and maybe the Old Folks would give a happy home to a new kitty that needed them. Whatever the future held, she would not be afraid. She decided that she would live happily ever after with the knowledge that the rainbow bridge would not be a scary place and that one day maybe she would see the old guy and the old gal at the rainbow bridge too.

EPILOG

GIZMO'S STORY

Gizmo became our kitty,
but for a time she was alone.
One day she just showed up
and made herself at home.

She was always very *skittish*,
seemed to find it hard to trust,
but we set up a feeding schedule
and slowly she began to adjust.

At first we couldn't pet her
she was having none of that,
but slowly, hand fed treats
brought some of her trust back

Eventually she would sit beside us,
but at first not in our lap,
she'd let us reach out to pet her,
but she was wary of being trapped.

She was always on the alert,
constantly well aware
and any sudden movement
would give her quite a scare.

For a time she fended for herself
trust seemed foreign to her
and though she was coming around,
we were yet to hear her purr.

When she first showed up
she wouldn't come into our home
and she'd disappear at night,
constantly off on the roam.

But after several months,
she learned we meant no harm.
Her resistance slowly faded
as the Old Gal turned on the charm.

We had coaxed her inside,
and allowed her to explore.
We didn't close her in
as constantly she eyed the door.

finally she came in every day
she thought she had us trained.
She had the run of the place
totally unrestrained.

She loved to lay in the window
always keeping track.
She was always on the lookout
always had our backs.

It was like she was protecting us,
from what we did not know,
but she'd stay an hour or more
until she'd get the urge to go.

She'd be back at dinner time
to grace us with her presence,
then it was out the door again,
it was an every night occurrence.

And every single morning
when we'd go out to get the paper,
She'd be there to have her breakfast
before heading out on another caper.

Like all pets do,
eventually Gizzy died,
but she'll never be forgotten
in our hearts she'll forever reside.

Untangling the web

attackofthecute.com

Do you love cute cat pics, dog photos and shots of ducks, rabbitsand more? Then here is a site for you. At thisblog you can swoon over a near-endless series of puppies, cubs and the like.Each photo lets you rate its pic on such criteria as "It's so cute" and "It's so fluffy"— and shots are easy to share via email, social media and more.

Made in the USA
Columbia, SC
10 November 2018